MW00899362

CONTENTS

About Me

Year	Age	Level

Favorite event to WATCH	Favorite Event to DO

Best event	Best skill

Most challenging event

Most challenging move

I can't wait until I can . . .

What I'm looking forward to this year

This season's goal is to

The skill I want to achieve this year

My Favorite thing to do at the gym

My Team

Strongest	Hardest Worker
Most Talkative	Most Supportive

My Coach always says

My Coach loves to make us

I look up to . . .	My Favorite gymnast

My Routine Skills

Floor	Pommel Horse
Vault	Still Rings
Parallel Bars	Horizontal Bar

Photo

MY SEASON
YEAR

MY MOST CONSISTENT
EVENT THIS SEASON WAS

Photo

My biggest achievement this season was

5

My Highest All Around Score	My Highest Event Score

I practiced

hours a week

days a week

I can hold a handstand for

seconds!

Photo

The Best thing about this season was . . .
Next season I'm going to . . .
Over the Summer I'm going to work on . . .

About Me

Year	Age	Level

Favorite event to WATCH	Favorite Event to DO
Best event	Best skill

Most challenging event

Most challenging move

I can't wait until I can . . .

What I'm looking forward to this year

This season's goal is to

The skill I want to achieve this year

My Favorite thing to do at the gym

My Team

Strongest	Hardest Worker
Most Talkative	Most Supportive

My Coach always says

My Coach loves to make us

I look up to . . .	My Favorite gymnast

My Routine Skills

Floor	Pommel Horse
Vault	Still Rings
Parallel Bars	Horizontal Bar

8

Photo

MY SEASON
YEAR

MY MOST CONSISTENT EVENT THIS SEASON WAS

Photo

My biggest achievement this season was

My Highest All Around Score	My Highest Event Score

I practiced

hours a week

days a week

Photo

I can hold a handstand for

seconds!

The Best thing about this season was . . .

Next season I'm going to . . .

Over the Summer I'm going to work on . . .

Meet			Date	Level	Age Div

Event	SCORE	Place
Floor		
Horse		
Rings		
Vault		
Parallel Bars		
Horizontal Bar		
All Around		

I did . . .	Floor	Horse	Rings	Vault	Parallel Bars	High Bar
THE BEST EVER!						
Better						
OK, The same						
I'll do better next time						

I STUCK MY LANDINGS

OH YEA   SORT OF   NOT QUITE

My Team Did Great

Name	Floor	Horse	Rings	Vault	Parallel Bars	High Bar

Team Score	Place

What I'm proud of this meet

For the next meet I'm going to work on . . .

Meet		Date	Level	Age Div

Event	SCORE	Place
Floor		
Horse		
Rings		
Vault		
Parallel Bars		
Horizontal Bar		
All Around		

I did . . .	Floor	Horse	Rings	Vault	Parallel Bars	High Bar
THE BEST EVER!						
Better						
OK, The same						
I'll do better next time						

I STUCK MY LANDINGS

OH YEA   SORT OF   NOT QUITE

My Team Did Great

Name	Floor	Horse	Rings	Vault	Parallel Bars	High Bar

Team Score	Place

What I'm proud of this meet

For the next meet I'm going to work on . . .

Meet		Date	Level	Age Div

Event	SCORE	Place
Floor		
Horse		
Rings		
Vault		
Parallel Bars		
Horizontal Bar		
All Around		

I did . . .	Floor	Horse	Rings	Vault	Parallel Bars	High Bar
THE BEST EVER!						
Better						
OK, The same						
I'll do better next time						

I STUCK MY LANDINGS

OH YEA   SORT OF   NOT QUITE

Name	Floor	Horse	Rings	Vault	Parallel Bars	High Bar

Team Score	Place

What I'm proud of this meet

For the next meet I'm going to work on . . .

Meet		Date	Level	Age Div

Event	SCORE	Place
Floor		
Horse		
Rings		
Vault		
Parallel Bars		
Horizontal Bar		
All Around		

I did . . .	Floor	Horse	Rings	Vault	Parallel Bars	High Bar
THE BEST EVER!						
Better						
OK, The same						
I'll do better next time						

I STUCK MY LANDINGS

OH YEA   SORT OF   NOT QUITE

My Team Did Great

Name	Floor	Horse	Rings	Vault	Parallel Bars	High Bar

Team Score	Place

What I'm proud of this meet

For the next meet I'm going to work on . . .

18

Meet				Date	Level	Age Div

Event	SCORE	Place
Floor		
Horse		
Rings		
Vault		
Parallel Bars		
Horizontal Bar		
All Around		

I did . . .	Floor	Horse	Rings	Vault	Parallel Bars	High Bar
THE BEST EVER!						
Better						
OK, The same						
I'll do better next time						

I STUCK MY LANDINGS

OH YEA   SORT OF   NOT QUITE

My Team Did Great

Name	Floor	Horse	Rings	Vault	Parallel Bars	High Bar

Team Score	Place

What I'm proud of this meet

For the next meet I'm going to work on . . .

Meet		Date	Level	Age Div

Event	SCORE	Place
Floor		
Horse		
Rings		
Vault		
Parallel Bars		
Horizontal Bar		
All Around		

I did . . .	Floor	Horse	Rings	Vault	Parallel Bars	High Bar
THE BEST EVER!						
Better						
OK, The same						
I'll do better next time						

I STUCK MY LANDINGS

OH YEA   SORT OF   NOT QUITE

My Team Did Great

Name	Floor	Horse	Rings	Vault	Parallel Bars	High Bar

Team Score	Place

What I'm proud of this meet

For the next meet I'm going to work on . . .

Meet				Date	Level	Age Div

Event	SCORE	Place
Floor		
Horse		
Rings		
Vault		
Parallel Bars		
Horizontal Bar		
All Around		

I did . . .	Floor	Horse	Rings	Vault	Parallel Bars	High Bar
THE BEST EVER!						
Better						
OK, The same						
I'll do better next time						

I STUCK MY LANDINGS

OH YEA   SORT OF   NOT QUITE

My Team Did Great

Name	Floor	Horse	Rings	Vault	Parallel Bars	High Bar

Team Score	Place

What I'm proud of this meet

For the next meet I'm going to work on . . .

Meet		Date	Level	Age Div

Event	SCORE	Place
Floor		
Horse		
Rings		
Vault		
Parallel Bars		
Horizontal Bar		
All Around		

I did . . .	Floor	Horse	Rings	Vault	Parallel Bars	High Bar
THE BEST EVER!						
Better						
OK, The same						
I'll do better next time						

I STUCK MY LANDINGS

OH YEA   SORT OF   NOT QUITE

My Team Did Great

Name	Floor	Horse	Rings	Vault	Parallel Bars	High Bar

Team Score	Place

What I'm proud of this meet

For the next meet I'm going to work on . . .

Meet		Date	Level	Age Div

Event	SCORE	Place
Floor		
Horse		
Rings		
Vault		
Parallel Bars		
Horizontal Bar		
All Around		

I did . . .	Floor	Horse	Rings	Vault	Parallel Bars	High Bar
THE BEST EVER!						
Better						
OK, The same						
I'll do better next time						

I STUCK MY LANDINGS

OH YEA   SORT OF   NOT QUITE

My Team Did Great

Name	Floor	Horse	Rings	Vault	Parallel Bars	High Bar

Team Score	Place

What I'm proud of this meet

For the next meet I'm going to work on . . .

Meet		Date	Level	Age Div

Event	SCORE	Place
Floor		
Horse		
Rings		
Vault		
Parallel Bars		
Horizontal Bar		
All Around		

I did . . .	Floor	Horse	Rings	Vault	Parallel Bars	High Bar
THE BEST EVER!						
Better						
OK, The same						
I'll do better next time						

I STUCK MY LANDINGS

OH YEA   SORT OF   NOT QUITE

My Team Did Great

Name	Floor	Horse	Rings	Vault	Parallel Bars	High Bar

Team Score	Place

What I'm proud of this meet

For the next meet I'm going to work on . . .

Meet		Date	Level	Age Div

Event	SCORE	Place
Floor		
Horse		
Rings		
Vault		
Parallel Bars		
Horizontal Bar		
All Around		

I did . . .	Floor	Horse	Rings	Vault	Parallel Bars	High Bar
THE BEST EVER!						
Better						
OK, The same						
I'll do better next time						

I STUCK MY LANDINGS

OH YEA   SORT OF   NOT QUITE

My Team Did Great

Name	Floor	Horse	Rings	Vault	Parallel Bars	High Bar

Team Score	Place

What I'm proud of this meet

For the next meet I'm going to work on . . .

Meet			Date	Level	Age Div

Event	SCORE	Place
Floor		
Horse		
Rings		
Vault		
Parallel Bars		
Horizontal Bar		
All Around		

I did . . .	Floor	Horse	Rings	Vault	Parallel Bars	High Bar
THE BEST EVER!						
Better						
OK, The same						
I'll do better next time						

I STUCK MY LANDINGS

OH YEA   SORT OF   NOT QUITE

My Team Did Great

Name	Floor	Horse	Rings	Vault	Parallel Bars	High Bar

Team Score	Place

What I'm proud of this meet

For the next meet I'm going to work on . . .

Meet				Date	Level	Age Div

Event	SCORE	Place
Floor		
Horse		
Rings		
Vault		
Parallel Bars		
Horizontal Bar		
All Around		

I did . . .	Floor	Horse	Rings	Vault	Parallel Bars	High Bar
THE BEST EVER!						
Better						
OK, The same						
I'll do better next time						

I STUCK MY LANDINGS

OH YEA   SORT OF   NOT QUITE

My Team Did Great

Name	Floor	Horse	Rings	Vault	Parallel Bars	High Bar

Team Score	Place

What I'm proud of this meet

For the next meet I'm going to work on . . .

Meet		Date	Level	Age Div

Event	SCORE	Place
Floor		
Horse		
Rings		
Vault		
Parallel Bars		
Horizontal Bar		
All Around		

I did . . .	Floor	Horse	Rings	Vault	Parallel Bars	High Bar
THE BEST EVER!						
Better						
OK, The same						
I'll do better next time						

I STUCK MY LANDINGS

OH YEA   SORT OF   NOT QUITE

My Team Did Great

Name	Floor	Horse	Rings	Vault	Parallel Bars	High Bar

Team Score	Place

What I'm proud of this meet

For the next meet I'm going to work on . . .

Meet		Date	Level	Age Div

Event	SCORE	Place
Floor		
Horse		
Rings		
Vault		
Parallel Bars		
Horizontal Bar		
All Around		

I did . . .	Floor	Horse	Rings	Vault	Parallel Bars	High Bar
THE BEST EVER!						
Better						
OK, The same						
I'll do better next time						

I STUCK MY LANDINGS

OH YEA   SORT OF   NOT QUITE

My Team Did Great

Name	Floor	Horse	Rings	Vault	Parallel Bars	High Bar

Team Score	Place

What I'm proud of this meet

For the next meet I'm going to work on . . .

Meet	Date	Level	Age Div

Event	SCORE	Place
Floor		
Horse		
Rings		
Vault		
Parallel Bars		
Horizontal Bar		
All Around		

I did . . .	Floor	Horse	Rings	Vault	Parallel Bars	High Bar
THE BEST EVER!						
Better						
OK, The same						
I'll do better next time						

I STUCK MY LANDINGS

OH YEA   SORT OF   NOT QUITE

My Team Did Great

Name	Floor	Horse	Rings	Vault	Parallel Bars	High Bar

Team Score	Place

What I'm proud of this meet

For the next meet I'm going to work on . . .

Meet		Date	Level	Age Div

Event	SCORE	Place
Floor		
Horse		
Rings		
Vault		
Parallel Bars		
Horizontal Bar		
All Around		

I did . . .	Floor	Horse	Rings	Vault	Parallel Bars	High Bar
THE BEST EVER!						
Better						
OK, The same						
I'll do better next time						

I STUCK MY LANDINGS

OH YEA   SORT OF   NOT QUITE

My Team Did Great

Name	Floor	Horse	Rings	Vault	Parallel Bars	High Bar

Team Score	Place

What I'm proud of this meet

For the next meet I'm going to work on . . .

44

Meet			Date	Level	Age Div

Event	SCORE	Place
Floor		
Horse		
Rings		
Vault		
Parallel Bars		
Horizontal Bar		
All Around		

I did . . .	Floor	Horse	Rings	Vault	Parallel Bars	High Bar
THE BEST EVER!						
Better						
OK, The same						
I'll do better next time						

I STUCK MY LANDINGS

OH YEA   SORT OF   NOT QUITE

My Team Did Great

Name	Floor	Horse	Rings	Vault	Parallel Bars	High Bar

Team Score	Place

What I'm proud of this meet

For the next meet I'm going to work on . . .

Meet		Date	Level	Age Div

Event	SCORE	Place
Floor		
Horse		
Rings		
Vault		
Parallel Bars		
Horizontal Bar		
All Around		

I did . . .	Floor	Horse	Rings	Vault	Parallel Bars	High Bar
THE BEST EVER!						
Better						
OK, The same						
I'll do better next time						

I STUCK MY LANDINGS

OH YEA   SORT OF   NOT QUITE

My Team Did Great

Name	Floor	Horse	Rings	Vault	Parallel Bars	High Bar

Team Score	Place

What I'm proud of this meet

For the next meet I'm going to work on . . .

Meet		Date	Level	Age Div

Event	SCORE	Place
Floor		
Horse		
Rings		
Vault		
Parallel Bars		
Horizontal Bar		
All Around		

I did . . .	Floor	Horse	Rings	Vault	Parallel Bars	High Bar
THE BEST EVER!						
Better						
OK, The same						
I'll do better next time						

I STUCK MY LANDINGS

OH YEA   SORT OF   NOT QUITE

My Team Did Great

Name	Floor	Horse	Rings	Vault	Parallel Bars	High Bar

Team Score	Place

What I'm proud of this meet

For the next meet I'm going to work on . . .

Meet		Date	Level	Age Div

Event	SCORE	Place
Floor		
Horse		
Rings		
Vault		
Parallel Bars		
Horizontal Bar		
All Around		

I did . . .	Floor	Horse	Rings	Vault	Parallel Bars	High Bar
THE BEST EVER!						
Better						
OK, The same						
I'll do better next time						

I STUCK MY LANDINGS

OH YEA   SORT OF   NOT QUITE

My Team Did Great

Name	Floor	Horse	Rings	Vault	Parallel Bars	High Bar

Team Score	Place

What I'm proud of this meet

For the next meet I'm going to work on . . .

Meet		Date	Level	Age Div

Event	SCORE	Place
Floor		
Horse		
Rings		
Vault		
Parallel Bars		
Horizontal Bar		
All Around		

I did . . .	Floor	Horse	Rings	Vault	Parallel Bars	High Bar
THE BEST EVER!						
Better						
OK, The same						
I'll do better next time						

I STUCK MY LANDINGS

OH YEA   SORT OF   NOT QUITE

My Team Did Great

Name	Floor	Horse	Rings	Vault	Parallel Bars	High Bar

Team Score	Place

What I'm proud of this meet

For the next meet I'm going to work on . . .

54

Meet		Date	Level	Age Div

Event	SCORE	Place
Floor		
Horse		
Rings		
Vault		
Parallel Bars		
Horizontal Bar		
All Around		

I did . . .	Floor	Horse	Rings	Vault	Parallel Bars	High Bar
THE BEST EVER!						
Better						
OK, The same						
I'll do better next time						

I STUCK MY LANDINGS

OH YEA   SORT OF   NOT QUITE

My Team Did Great

Name	Floor	Horse	Rings	Vault	Parallel Bars	High Bar

Team Score	Place

What I'm proud of this meet

For the next meet I'm going to work on . . .

Meet		Date	Level	Age Div

Event	SCORE	Place
Floor		
Horse		
Rings		
Vault		
Parallel Bars		
Horizontal Bar		
All Around		

I did . . .	Floor	Horse	Rings	Vault	Parallel Bars	High Bar
THE BEST EVER!						
Better						
OK, The same						
I'll do better next time						

I STUCK MY LANDINGS

OH YEA   SORT OF   NOT QUITE

My Team Did Great

Name	Floor	Horse	Rings	Vault	Parallel Bars	High Bar

Team Score	Place

What I'm proud of this meet

For the next meet I'm going to work on . . .

Meet			Date	Level	Age Div

Event	SCORE	Place
Floor		
Horse		
Rings		
Vault		
Parallel Bars		
Horizontal Bar		
All Around		

I did . . .	Floor	Horse	Rings	Vault	Parallel Bars	High Bar
THE BEST EVER!						
Better						
OK, The same						
I'll do better next time						

I STUCK MY LANDINGS

OH YEA   SORT OF   NOT QUITE

My Team Did Great

Name	Floor	Horse	Rings	Vault	Parallel Bars	High Bar

Team Score	Place

What I'm proud of this meet

For the next meet I'm going to work on . . .

GOALS

Date	Goal	Date Achieved

Date	Skill	Details

Personal Best

Enter only your highest score.
Each entry should be higher than the last

Floor		Pommel Horse		Still Rings	
Date	Score	Date	Score	Date	Score

Personal Best

Enter only your highest score.
Each entry should be higher than the last

Vault		Parallel Bars		High Bar	
Date	Score	Date	Score	Date	Score

Floor Scores

Date	Meet	Level	Score	Place

Pommel Horse Scores

Date	Meet	Level	Score	Place

66

Still Rings Scores

Date	Meet	Level	Score	Place

Vault Scores

Date	Meet	Level	Score	Place

Parallel Bars Scores

Date	Meet	Level	Score	Place

Horizontal Bar Scores

Date	Meet	Level	Score	Place

My All Around Scores

Date	Level	Age Division	Score	Place

Contacts

Name	Phone	E-Mail	Parents Name

My Gym

Address

Phone Number

Fax

E-mail

Web address

The best thing about my gym is ...